1210

My Senses

Leon Read

W
FRANKLIN WATTS
LONDON • SYDNEY

Contents

Look out for Tiger on the pages of this book. Sometimes he is hiding.

We have five senses.

hearing

seeing

tasting

touching

smelling

Seeing

We see things with our eyes.

What are you using your eyes for now?

4

Billy wears glasses.

His sight is blurry without them.

When it's dark

It is hard to see in the dark.

I like the dark.
I play with
my torch.

We need light to see.

What other things light up the dark?

Hearing

We hear sounds
with our ears.

Hearing aids

Some people
need help to
hear sounds.

Sounds around

We hear sounds
almost all the time.

tweet tweet

tweet tweet

I recorded some
of my favourite
sounds.

Touching

We touch with our skin.
Our fingers are good
at feeling things.

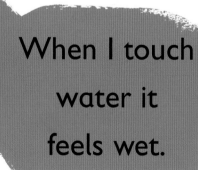

When I touch
water it
feels wet.

Billy and Grace
like Tiger.
He feels soft.

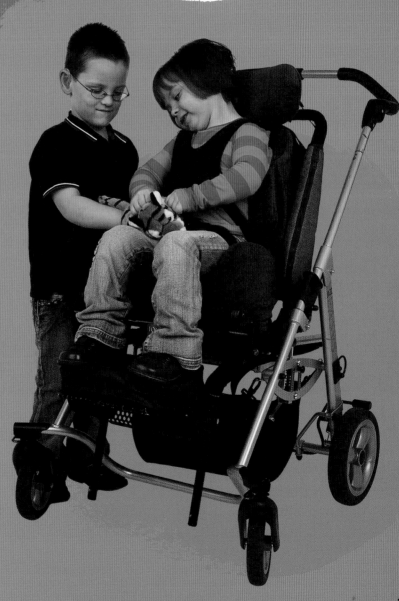

Smelling

We smell things
with our nose.

Some things smell nice.

foamy soap

Some things smell bad.

stinky sock

15

Smell and tell

Smelling things helps us to tell what they are. You can play a fruit smelling game.

I mixed up the boxes. Then I guessed which fruit was in each box.

Tasting

We taste food and drink
with our tongue.

This is a list of all my favourite tastes.

What are your favourite tastes?

Staying safe

Our senses help us to stay safe.

How do our senses help us to stay safe in a busy street?

How do our senses
tell us when food is
not safe to eat?

I took a photo
of some stinky,
mouldy cheese.

21

Super senses

tasting

smelling

seeing

We have
five senses.

hearing

touching

Alex is making a
senses collage.

Find pictures
in old
magazines
and make a
collage of
your own.

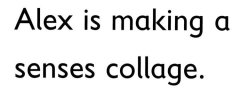

Word picture bank

Glasses – P. 5

Hearing aid – P. 9

Light – P. 7

Mouldy – P. 21

Stinky – P. 15

Wet – P. 12

First published in 2007 by Franklin Watts
338 Euston Road, London NW1 3BH

Franklin Watts Australia
Level 17/207 Kent Street, Sydney NSW 2000

Copyright © Franklin Watts 2007

Series editor: Adrian Cole
Photographer: Andy Crawford
Design: Sphere Design Associates
Art director: Jonathan Hair
Consultants: Prue Goodwin and Karina Law

A CIP catalogue record for this book is available
from the British Library.

ISBN: 978 0 7496 7615 5

Dewey Classification: 612.8

Acknowledgements:
The Publisher would like to thank Norrie Carr model agency
and Scope. 'Tiger' puppet used with kind permission from
Ravensden PLC (www.ravensden.co.uk).
Tiger Talk logo drawn by Kevin Hopgood.

Every attempt has been made to clear copyright. Should there
be any inadvertent omission please apply to the publisher for
rectification.

Printed in China

Franklin Watts is a division
of Hachette Children's Books,
an Hachette Livre UK company.

There are 18 Tigers, including me, in this book. Did you find all of us?

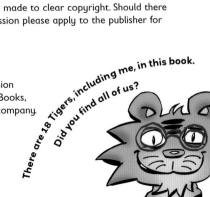